FIFTY WAYS TO TEACH READING
Tips for ESL/EFL Teachers

SHANE DIXON

CONTENTS

HOW TO USE THIS BOOK

The activities in this book are organized into these categories:

- pre-reading
- reading
- post-reading
- intensive
- extensive

Pre-reading activities focus on preparing and intriguing learners by providing material that helps them gain insights and context about what they will read.

Reading activities occur during a reading, and invite learners to find material that will help them comprehend the text more readily. Some of these reading activities must be given ahead of time so that learners can read and work on their own, but other reading activities involve stopping midway during a reading, either with the teacher or with a group or partner.

Post-reading activities give learners a chance to demonstrate their comprehension of the reading, and often serve as evaluative or critical thinking instruments – to see what students know and feel about a reading.

Intensive reading is a detailed, top-down approach to reading with specific language tasks.

In contrast, **extensive reading** involves reading texts for enjoyment, often autonomously, to develop general reading skills. Whereas intensive readings are often chosen by teachers, extensive readings are often chosen by learners. Intensive reading has a specific learner strategy or goal in mind, and the goal of extensive reading is to encourage learners to "get lost" in the experience of reading.

As you read the following activities, keep in mind these suggestions:

- Read all fifty tips and become familiar with each of them.
- For a balanced approach, use a different focus (language, meaning, or literary) from your last reading, or consider multiple activities for one reading (at least one language, meaning, and literary focus for each reading).

INTRODUCTION

This book is for teachers both new and experienced to the world of Teaching English to Speakers of Other Languages (TESOL). The activities here are deliberately both simple and common. This provides two distinct advantages. First, you can modify these activities to suit your own needs and context. Second, this small book can remind you of activities you once used and loved, but may have forgotten.

As you choose an activity in this book, consider first the purpose of the reading. As is always the case in instruction, purpose should drive selection. If you have more than one purpose, consider your primary focus.

For example, for some teachers, the primary purpose for a reading is to introduce learners to vocabulary, sentence structure, parts of speech, and even pronunciation. These teachers have a **language focus**. In contrast, others see readings as an opportunity to have a **meaning focus,** helping learners to discuss main ideas, share opinions, and engage in critical thinking. Still other teachers might have a **literary focus**, where they invite learners to identify character, plot, setting, metaphor, and other literary devices.

We believe that many of the activities presented here can, with a little teacher creativity, be modified not only to suit the above concepts but your own focus as well.

Where to Find Reading Materials

Colleagues. Look to high-energy teachers who inspire you and ask them to share the readings that they have used with great success.

- **Textbooks**. Textbooks often are organized according to high interest themes and are leveled according to the language proficiency of your learners.
- **Students**. Don't forget to include your students in your quest to find great reading material. You may find that students are naturally finding materials that engage and motivate them.
- **Your own experience**. Don't forget the general truth that what *you* find interesting and fascinating is simply easier to teach. If you are inspired by the reading, it is more likely that your enthusiasm will rub off.
- **Language approach**. Consider what language you want your learners to be able to use. For example, if you want learners to understand the passive voice, you might select a reading about history that talks about when a city was built or how it was developed.

- **Reading approach**. You may wish to do the opposite of a language approach. In other words, find a reading that you find intriguing and then look for language that, at your students' level, might be worthwhile to teach.

PRE-READING ACTIVITIES

Pre-reading activities help learners by reducing the cogni-
tive load (or reading difficulty) or the passages they are

given, and are, as the name suggests, to students before any reading is done.

Pre-reading activities are essential to learners in several ways. First, pre-reading skills allow students to activate their previous knowledge of the subject matter. In other words, if students are going to read about the Australian outback, pre-reading strategies often allow students to discuss and share what they already know and understand about the outback.

Furthermore, pre-reading activities allow students to build information that will assist in the reading process, giving needed vocabulary and cultural context to assist in the reading process.

Finally, pre-reading activities are a great boon to motivation, providing learners with opportunities to imagine, predict, and conceptualize what they are about to read. Good pre-reading activities, in short, make learners want to read the material that is about to be presented, and can be a tool to help learners visualize and think critically.

INFORMATION GAP

This term describes a variety of language activities with one common feature: one person or group of people has information that others do not have. The point of an information gap activity is to have people interact with each other to find all the missing information.

For example, one student might have a map with all of the rivers labeled with all the mountains are unlabeled. Another student has a map that is precisely the reverse, with all of the mountains labeled but not the rivers. Students with the river map are not allowed to look at the mountain map, and students with the mountain map are not allowed to look at the river map. Instructions are given that students are not allowed to look at each other's map. Thus, students must complete their maps with both rivers and mountains by talking with each other and asking questions.

While information gap activities can be used in a variety of ways, as a pre-reading activity, they can help to stimulate conversation and help students gain immediate access to themes and vocabulary useful to a reading. In the example above about maps, for example, an information gap about a particular location that has rivers and mountains might prompt students to remember or learn key vocabulary that the reading presents.

SENTENCE STARTERS

Sentence starters give students a chance to practice vocabulary and grammatical structures. Sentence starters are prompts that invite students to finish a sentence; for example, *When I am old, I will...* or *My favorite sport is...* .

By inviting students to finish one or a series of sentence starters, students will key in on the themes, vocabulary, and, with careful prompts, even the grammatical structure of a reading.

Sentence starters also give students a chance to share their knowledge with each other, which often provides the kind of interaction that promotes real learning. Since students of the same age/classroom/level tend to think and respond in unique yet similar ways, the interaction allows them to learn from each other in a more natural way than textbook learning.

Sentence starters might be given by writing them on the

board or through a handout. You might even ask students to come up with their own after modeling a few. Regardless of how you structure the sentence starters, you should invite students in pairs or groups to share their completed sentences.

❧ 3 ❧

TWO-MINUTE DEBATE

Debates can help stimulate conversation about topics presented in a reading. While debates might be introduced after a reading as well, a simple debate format can provoke interest in a topic and get students thinking about difficult, open-ended questions.

Debates may be a bit much for basic and intermediate classes, although they can still be done if given proper instructions and simple prompts. (*Breakfast is an important meal. / Teenagers need less sleep than adults.*)

Divide the class in pairs and tell them that they will be given a simple statement or series of statements to debate. You might have students divide themselves according to how they would naturally answer, or you could divide students yourself.

In the latter format, Student A would agree with the statement, and Student B would disagree. The strength of this format is that it encourages students to think critically of positions outside of their own. In this format, you can carefully prepare questions about the reading topic that allow for opposing viewpoints.

Give students a few minutes to think of arguments. Circulate while students are working to answer vocabulary questions. You may wish to allow bilingual dictionaries at this stage too.

Explain that Student A will have the first minute to share thoughts and Student B will have the second minute. Remind students that they don't have to personally agree with their assigned position; rather, they are presenting the arguments for that point of view.

Ask students to continue speaking even if they feel they have nothing to say (perhaps through phrases for hesitation or repetition of their previous sentence).

As a wrap-up, show the class the title of the reading and ask which of the arguments they gave (or heard) they believe will show up in the reading. This kind of prediction exercise increases motivation to read.

❧ 4 ❧
PERSON PREDICTION (AUTHOR OR CHARACTER)

Inviting learners to predict is a powerful motivational tool that helps to naturally elicit vocabulary and interest in potential themes.

One way to inspire this kind of interest is by exposing students to the author or characters of a reading. Inviting students to predict the content of a reading based on a small biography or character sketch allows students to learn how to piece context clues together and inspire them to match their guesses to the actual reading.

To do an activity of this nature, consider bringing in a picture of an author or a character. Alternatively, you could bring in a short biography that gives a few clues; or, at an advanced level, provide pictures and short biographies of several characters and ask students to match them up. At the most basic level, however, you can invite learners to guess what that character might be like.

For example, you might ask them to consider if the person

is a hero, a villain, a minor or major character. Ask them to consider the person's hobbies, occupation, likes/dislikes, dreams, and even problems. Invite learners to share some of their written opinions.

The reading should naturally cover the answers from the questions you make, so be sure your questions take into account the reading you assigned!

PICTURE PREDICTION

Inviting learners to predict is a powerful motivational tool that helps to naturally elicit vocabulary and interest in potential themes. One of the ways to inspire this kind of interest is by exposing students to pictures that depict scenes or characters relevant to the reading.

For example, a reading about the Great Depression might demonstrate several pictures that demonstrate families or individuals that lived in the Great Depression. Choosing iconic or interesting actions often helps students to discuss or share ideas about what they imagine to be in the picture.

By giving students a picture and asking them to respond, you will be eliciting vocabulary or grammar from them. Have students look for vocabulary words, possibly in pairs or groups, or even writing down key vocabulary words they might need to accomplish their description. Asking learners to describe the scene and then reading later to see the accuracy of their prediction is motivating to must students.

The most important part of this activity is choosing a picture that reveals detail, but not too many details of the reading, which inspires learners to want to know more.

ROLE PLAY

One way to intrigue learners about a particular topic is to have them role play. Role play stimulates the creative centers of the brain and allows for quick decisions, humor, and fun.

When using role play as a pre-reading activity, it is best to set the scene for students by describing certain characters or situations. You might even have students select fellow class members for the roles as you read out short descriptions (*This is a character who is really strong...who do you think could play this character?*).

You might, however, invite members to choose themselves if there are negative characteristics (*Is there anyone here who likes to pretend to be the villain? Who wants to be the bad guy today?*) Alternatively, you could play the villain yourself, or you could select someone whose character is not in question among other class members.

After establishing roles, give each student small speaking

tasks that provide them an opportunity to negotiate meaning or accomplish a task. For example, one learner might be a flight attendant, and another learner a passenger, and they might need to figure out how to land a plane that lost its pilot. The teacher gives instructions and the students listen and try to follow along. Giving students a scenario to act out can be fun and educational.

PREDICT FROM A TITLE

Have students read the title of the reading and then predict what the text will be about. This will increase motivation to read because students naturally want to see if they were correct. It will also bring relevant vocabulary to the fore as they discuss their guesses.

Give students time to discuss different possibilities, and help them elaborate on those possibilities. For example, if the title is *Danger in the Desert*, students might speculate who is in danger, what the danger is, and what might happen as a result.

An accompanying picture or even group of pictures can stimulate even more conversation. You might reveal certain clues as students form their opinions, and then have them change their opinions as certain clues get revealed.

If students get stuck in coming up with information, you might ask them to compose answers based on the most basic question words such as *Who* / *What* / *Why* / *When* / *Where* / *How*.

After the reading, discuss which predictions were the most accurate, and let the students who made those predictions explain how they made their guesses.

STORY GUESSWORK

Similar to the activity found in Tip #6, *Predict from a Title*, this activity allows students to take a sneak peak and make guesses about the content based on the information or clues given. In this case, students are able to read an entire first section (which could be the first paragraph or a series of paragraphs).

After students read the first section, they guess what the story or reading will be about. A clever teacher might give a handout with carefully planned questions about certain characters, places, or details. Encourage students to use both clues in what they've read and their general knowledge about story genre or the topic to inform their guesses.

Guessing a storyline can intrigue students and get them thinking about key vocabulary. You can gamify this activity by having students "lock in" their answers, and then revealing the correct answer or group of answers at the end of the reading. Students who guess the most correct answers win.

❧ II ❧
READING ACTIVITIES

When we discuss reading activities, sometimes teachers are confused about what exactly "reading activities" mean. Some teachers assume that reading IS the activity, with pre-reading and post-reading activities to supplement it. *Students, sit quietly at your desk and read* is the stereotypical perspective of this teacher.

While it is true that reading, and reading by yourself, is indeed an activity unto itself, good teachers know that reading can be so much more. There are many different types of reading according to style (individual, pair, or group) as well as a number of different strategies that typically accompany reading (scanning, skimming, or reading for main ideas).

Yet another way to think of reading activities is by the number of sub-activities that accompany a reading. These activities promote critical thinking and motivation, helping readers to recognize various ways to imagine the reading process. Many of these activities break up a reading into more manageable chunks, giving students a chance to interact with others or the text itself in interesting ways. Above all, these kinds of reading activities, done *within* a reading, make reading enjoyable.

STOP AND PREDICT

This reading activity breaks up a text into different sections, and can be particularly useful when reading together with a class, when a text is large, or any other time when stopping might be considered necessary (like during a cliff hanger).

When reading together, stop students at a part of the reading that elicits a response, and have them guess what might happen next. Get several viewpoints and possibilities of what will probably happen, or ask the class to discuss which ending is most likely or most desirable. You might write answers on the board and even vote on those answers.

Be sure to come back and discuss the predictions once the correct answers are known.

COLLOCATIONAL RELATIONSHIPS

Help students find the natural relationships that exist among words.

For example, take two words from a reading, such as the words *bear* and *honey* from a Winnie the Pooh story. Students draw two arrows between *bear* and *honey*. Students then have to consider the relationship from *bear* to *honey* (with the arrow pointing from *bear* to *honey*) and the relationship from *honey* to *bear* (with the arrow pointing from *honey* to *bear*). Have them express these relationships in writing. Students should use words/sentences that make the relationship clear.

Sentences from *bear* to *honey*:

> *Bears like honey. Bears are happy when they eat honey.*
> *Bears eat honey.*

Sentences from *honey* to *bear*:

Honey pleases bears. Honey makes bears happy. Honey is a treasure for bears.

Finally, have students create sentences that might be similar using different characters or words from the book. (*Rabbits don't like honey. Rabbits like carrots.*)

READ ALOUD

This activity gives learners the chance to comprehend a reading by hearing it read aloud by the teacher, a partner, or a small group. Read-aloud activities give opportunities for a teacher to teach different learners a variety of strategies for reading, listening, and speaking.

Before a read-aloud, learners may be given a sheet of questions to answer, a list of vocabulary words to look for, or another language task.

Here are some tips for a successful teacher-directed read-aloud:

- Choose a story that students love or relate to
- Stand in front of the class and have every student open to the same page.
- Read in a dynamic voice.
- Pause often and stimulate interest by asking students to predict.

- Have students read along to various parts, especially exciting parts.
- Watch a movie clip version after you have read a particular chapter.

Within the technique of reading aloud are a number of excellent teacher techniques. Consider using several of the following each time you do a read-aloud:

- **Choral Reading**: All participants read aloud and all together.
- **One by One and Sentence by Sentence**: Each person reads a sentence.
- **Dramatic Reading**: Focus on emotions and feelings.
- **Physical Response Reading**: Describe and act out physical actions and movements.
- **Paired Reading**: Each partner reads one sentence/paragraph at a time.
- **The Leader and the Choral Response**: The leader reads one sentence, and then the large group echoes back that sentence (or the large group might read the next sentence). Then alternate back and forth between the leader and the group reading a sentence out loud.
- **Small Group Reading**: In small groups, form circles and have each student read a sentence, going around the circle.
- **Male and Female Roles or Turn**s: All the women read one sentence and the men read the next one; or take turns reading the dialog for women and for men.

- **Fill in the Missing/Silent Words**: The leader reads aloud and pauses in the sentence for the group to fill in the words that are the focus of vocabulary or pronunciation practice.
- **Silent Reading**: Everyone reads a paragraph or page silently. Then ask questions about the reading or vocabulary, etc.
- **Listen and Read**: Participants watch part of a movie version of the book and then read the same portion of the story (this is a good review and a way to cover more difficult passages twice for better comprehension).
- **Read and Listen**: Participants read a passage in the book and then review the same part in the movie (this is a good way to focus on listening to dialog, vocabulary, grammar, and comprehension).
- **Read and Discuss**: The leader of a small group asks questions about the reading or how the other group members feel about a topic or idea presented in the book or movie.
- **Read and Write**: Participants write book reports or short essays in class.

JIGSAWS

Jigsaw readings allow students to interact with members of two different groups, and provides a chance to both learn from others and lead.

Divide the classroom into four groups (A, B, C, and D). Divide a reading into four parts, with one part for each group (so group A reads part A). The students in each group read and take notes on their respective part.

After each group has finished reading, students form new groups, with one member from each original group represented (so a member of A, B, C, and D all sit down together). In this group formation, each student is now the only one who has read the part assigned.

Students now report information to the members of the new group. Every student takes notes on the other sections of the reading. This gives every student the chance to be a reader, a speaker, and a listener, which naturally encourages interaction.

Often when using a jigsaw reading, the teacher provides questions that the final groups must answer, and should monitor each group to provide guidance and answer questions.

DETAIL DISCOVERY

This activity requires the teacher to create a handout or place a list of 10 questions on the board, and serves as a way to guide students through the material in a deliberate fashion. It is, at its core, a scanning activity, inviting students to look through the material for specific details.

This is done by giving learners, either through a handout or on the board, a list of true/false statements about information found in a reading. You might consider, for example, creating ten questions. These could be open ended or true/false.

Another way, however, to do this activity is to invite students to come up with 10 details (or any number, really) based on a single question (*How does the mother show love to her son in this story?*).

❧ 14 ❧

FIND A WORD

Write a definition of a word on the board without the word itself. Have students look for the word in the reading that has this particular meaning. This can be done as students are reading, thereby keeping them alert while reading.

For example, if the word is *representative*, you might write, "a person chosen or appointed to act or speak for another or others."

You can invite students to locate where the answer is found in the text, write the answers on a separate piece of paper, or meet in groups to find the location of each word.

This type of activity helps students improve their scanning skills. You could also use this same technique for other purposes: ask students to search for a main idea, a sentence that reminds them of a story, a sentence that they disagree with, and so on.

READING WITH HALF THE WORDS

Since many readings offer a number of words students don't know, this exercise helps students realize they don't need to know every word in order to understand general meaning. This activity also helps students understand the importance of inferring the meaning of a word or sentence from context.

Remove half of the words of a text by cutting a story or article in half vertically, or ask students to cover half of the reading with another piece of paper.

Now with only half of the words visible, students try to guess what the reading is talking about. You can assist by asking a series of questions about the article to help students guess the meaning. Then show the rest of the article and have students discuss how well they were able to predict.

Variation: Make this reading activity an information gap, giving student A half of the reading and student B the other half. The goal of the activity is always to answer the reading comprehension questions that the teacher has created for the activity.

Half-Reading

Part 1 Directions: Read this article and answer the questions provided below. Then read the full article and see how well you were able to infer the answers.

> **Questions 1-2 are based
> passage.**
>
> Early scientist belie
> dinosaurs, like most reptil
> immediately abandoned tl
> hatched young were left t
> themselves. However, the
> group of nests has challer
> nests, which contained fo
> dinosaurs they were not u
> evidence that dinosaur pa
> for their young. For some
> babies stayed at the nest v
> brought back plant matter
> stayed at home until they
> roam safely on their own.

1. What did scientists used to believe about dinosaurs?
2. What did the newly hatched young have to do?
3. What do scientists believe now about dinosaurs?

FOCUS ON ORGANIZATION

This reading activity works when there is a clear-cut organization (and organizational purpose) to the reading.

For fiction writing, you might have students look at exposition, rising action, climax, falling action, and denouement. Invite students to identify and summarize these different sections. This can happen by numbering the paragraphs in a separate handout and then providing a list of questions that accompany the numbered paragraphs (e.g., *In what paragraph is the climax found?*).

For non-fiction writing, try having students identify main topics and subtopics, getting them to consider the logic behind the overall structure.

To help students see the structure of a non-fiction reading, you could create a simple outline that allows students to follow along. For example, you could show students that a main idea often has two or three ideas that serve as support or evidence. For less advanced students, you could fill out a portion of the outline with them.

After filling out the handout (either for fiction or non-fiction), have students discuss their results and demonstrate their knowledge in pairs, groups, or to the entire class.

FOCUS ON A LITERARY
TECHNIQUE

An interesting reading activity can involve taking students through a reading to demonstrate a particular literary technique. Language teachers can learn a lot from literature teachers, who often help students recognize and understand metaphors, similes, rhymes, color imagery, description, setting, plot, allusion, and other literary devices.

For example, even basic learners can be given questions about the symbols found in nursery rhymes. In *Little Red Riding Hood*, you can ask students why they think the author chose a wolf as the animal, why the protagonist wears a cape, and what the message of the story is.

In short, don't ever be afraid to teach good literary techniques as well as language. It helps students appreciate the beauty of another language, and will certainly help them to engage with reading.

❧ III ❧
POST-READING
ACTIVITIES

Teachers naturally love to read, and naturally love to talk about the things they read, so most teachers understand the importance—and joy—of post-reading activities. This is your chance to get students into the material, to see themselves in the material, and to learn from it.

Good post-reading activities can prompt vocabulary and grammar instruction, but can also prompt communication, motivation, self-discovery, and greater knowledge about the world, not to mention that post-reading activities can be a lot of fun.

Here we present a few post-reading activities that are considered favorites among ESL and EFL instructors. Please notice that many of these activities can be slightly changed according to your purpose. Remember that as you select an activity, you must first decide if it fits your goal. For example, are you trying to get students speaking, thinking, or understanding language? Once you know your goal, you will see the activity as a means to achieve it, and will be able to select or modify the activity accordingly.

STRING QUESTIONING

This is a communicative activity through and through, although it might be modified to accomplish almost any goal. String questioning is a deliberate attempt to make asking questions more enjoyable through movement. After students get the point of the game, you will be amazed at how much fun they have. Here is how it works.

This question and answer game is best done by telling students that they will answer questions immediately after reading in a circle aloud to each other.

Students are placed in the circle, and one student is selected to hold a ball of yarn. Explain to students that only the student who is holding onto the ball of yarn may answer a question.

Then give that student a question (prepared in advance) about a reading. The student will respond and then take the ball of yarn with one hand and hold the end of the string with the other. The student will keep the end of the string and throw the ball, creating a line between the first and second student.

When the second student catches the ball, ask a second question. If a student makes an incorrect answer, you can decide whether to have that student answer another question or if they can pass the ball of yarn to another student. Make sure that the string between each student is tight, like a line, connecting everyone together. Eventually the string forms a web.

FINISH/REWRITE THE STORY

This post-reading activity is especially applicable to fiction stories or nonfiction that demonstrates a future need or cause.

After students finish reading a story or article, ask them to consider the question *What happens next?* Invite them to write a final chapter or a continuation to the story or article. This will give students the ability to think about the natural conclusions that can be made from a story, and can provide a creative outlet.

If it is a nonfiction article, invite students to think of what will likely happen in the recent or even distant future.

This activity can be done in pairs, groups, or individually.

Variation: Have students read all but the end of a story and then write their own endings. After these are shared with the class, read the original ending. Finish with a discussion of similarities and differences between the students' endings and the original author's ending.

20

TALKING TOKENS

Some students tend to be shy when it comes to speaking, and let a few students dominate the discussion. This technique allows for a more even distribution of participation, without a teacher having to pay so much attention to who has/has not spoken.

Before or after the reading, have students grab a number of tokens. You may or may not wish to explain what they are for (it can be fun to keep the purpose of the tokens a secret). A token might be a small coin, a marble, a piece of candy, or any sort of small item that can be quickly distributed.

After the reading, invite students to participate in a discussion. However, now explain that the tokens represent one opportunity to speak, and that every student must speak as many times as they have tokens. If your "token" is a candy, such as an M&M, students may only eat one after they make a comment.

Each token will stand for one time a student is required to speak. Explain that as soon as their tokens run out, students are required to listen to other learners. This technique encourages students to participate, and prevents having just a few students answer all the questions.

The second time you use this technique, distribute the tokens yourself, more or less evenly (or even exactly evenly). Don't make it look like you are withholding opportunities for eager students to speak or forcing quiet ones to speak more, but just giving all class members opportunities to speak without taking over the discussion.

21

CHARACTER MAPS

One way to involve students in reading is to have them choose a favorite character. Having students select someone in a story that resonates with them creates more motivation and allows them to examine similarities and differences between the character and themselves.

After inviting students to choose a character, there are several activities that can help deepen their understanding of the story. One activity is a character map. A character map might give a brief description of the character and visually display elements about him or her.

For example, the teacher could have students draw a picture of the character and add symbols and details to describe the character's physical characteristics, personality, and struggles or problems.

This can be a predictive activity as well, and you can ask students what they hope will happen to the character and/or what they think will happen to the character later on. It can also help to identify motives and recognize fatal flaws, or serve as a way to discuss both positive and negative aspects about a character's personality.

A reader might also be invited to draw a map about him or herself in comparison or contrast to the character.

PICTURE AND PRESENT

This activity allows students to choose a favorite portion of the book and share about that portion. This increases engagement and motivation, and makes sharing less of a chore. It also allows students to create something visually interesting, which is good for creative learners and useful in making presentations livelier.

The idea behind picture and present is simple. Upon finishing a reading, have students create a single picture that describes a scene, character, or detail from the story.

Students then present the picture to a partner or a group, and discuss why they drew the picture. This might be done in groups, pairs, or individually. If your classroom allows for it, display the pictures around the room until you have finished working with the book.

CIRCLE THE CORRECT WORD

This is an activity that can serve to help students recall what was in a reading, or to simply enjoy how simple words can change the entire meaning of a story.

To create a "circle the correct word" activity, you must first take a portion of a reading. You will then select key vocabulary words, meaning words upon which the entire meaning of the story resides. These words can be replaced with a pair of words: one is the correct word, and the other is a distractor/false choice. Students are required to circle what they believe is the correct word.

Example:

*In the **middle/top** of the night, many **constellations/confrontations** appear in the sky, and **stargazers/starblazers** of old imagined a world of **mythical/methodical** gods and goddesses.*

As a variation, you might invite students to create their own activity, replacing words with false choices. Having students come up with false choices can be entertaining and educational!

24

RANK ORDER IDEAS

Have students read and take notes about ideas that seem important (for example, *What are the most important ideas/themes from this reading?*). This could be the main themes of the reading, the moral of the reading, or just a list of details. It is best if students write full sentences for each item they list (instead of writing *child poverty*, for example, ask students to write, *Children often live in poverty in Brazilian favelas*).

Then, after students have created a list of ideas (either on the board or on a piece of paper), give them a "ranking form" (see example below) and invite students to rank the ideas in order of importance. Afterwards, have students share how they ordered the ideas with a partner, a group, or the class.

Rank Order Exercise

Directions: While you are reading, write down the ideas that seem most important to you. After you finish reading, decide which ideas are most importantor most interesting. Put the most important or interesting point first, then the second, third, fourth, and so on. Be prepared to discuss why you put these ideas in this order.

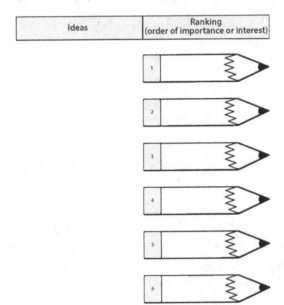

Ideas	Ranking (order of importance or interest)

ALPHABET READING

This activity is an excellent one to help students review, and can be used to help students prepare for a quiz.

While students are reading, write each letter of the alphabet on the board, with a space after each letter to write a small response. Then have students recall as many facts as they can that start with each letter (For example, *Apricots were John's favorite fruit. Betty didn't like John.*)

As a variation, you could provide a sheet of paper with each letter of the alphabet. Students complete the worksheet individually or in groups. If you wish to make it competitive, the student or group with the most responses in a given time frame wins.

GAP FILL OR CLOZE PASSAGE

This activity is an excellent one to help students recall and review material they have just read.

After students read a passage, take the passage or a portion of the passage and remove some of the words in a basic fill-in-the-blank format; then instruct students to fill in the blanks with the correct words. You can provide a word bank if students need more support.

One way to make this activity more entertaining is by providing false words instead of the real words, and having students identify and correct the false words. This is similar to the paired choice activity "Circle the Correct Word" (see tip #23).

If you create a word bank for students to choose from, add several incorrect choices there as well. Then students have to really consider each word, and cannot rely on the process of elimination to complete the final few gaps.

WORD SEARCH

Create a word search or crossword puzzle based on the vocabulary words of the reading. A word search has rows and columns of letters. Words may appear horizontally, vertically, diagonally, and go both forwards and backwards. For a free word search generator, try http://www.puzzlemaker.com/WS/

Word searches are especially useful in two particular contexts. First, as a review tool: When students need to review vocabulary (for a quiz or as part of a larger assignment), a word search can help students to recognize the words necessary to be successful on the quiz or assignment. It reinforces both spelling and scanning skills.

Another use, however, is as a sponge activity. Since some students are faster than others at completing a task, a word search can often help reinforce the ideas of the lesson and allow faster students some opportunity for additional practice. Slower students can then take home the word search for additional practice—a fun activity becomes a reward, not a punishment or 'homework.'

QUESTIONS IN A HAT

One of the biggest difficulties that teachers have is in creating a variety of questions based on the assignments/readings/lectures that students are required to accomplish. This activity allows teachers to enlist the help of the students, and also invites students to think critically about the reading.

Rather than writing all the test questions yourself, ask students to write test questions on cards or slips of paper about a reading the class has done. Place the questions in a hat. Then select some of the best questions learners have come up with for a future quiz.

This activity not only helps you to generate test question ideas, it will also allow students to think critically about the main ideas and important details of the content they are learning.

29

INTERVIEW WRITING

Generating ideas is one of the most important elements of writing. Sometimes students have difficulty generating ideas until they engage in discussion with their peers. Thus, one of the best things students can do is start listening to others.

In this activity, have students interview each other about their feelings or understanding of a reading. Invite them to come up with questions on their own, or create a series of questions to help guide an interview.

If you are particularly worried that students will not come up with any questions on their own, spend some time creating questions with them. Encourage students to ask questions that might elicit answers beyond yes/no by asking them to make sure their questions are open ended. You may need to provide a few examples (such as, *Why did you argue with your father?* instead of *Did you argue with your father?*).

You might also invite students to reflect on questions that might be more than informational, such as application questions or personal reflection questions.

30

SURVEY WRITING

Do you want to provide opportunities for students to respond to a reading critically or personally? One of the simplest ways to encourage student response after a reading is to have students conduct surveys among themselves.

Surveys can be created online or through the use of a handout or questions on the board.

At more basic levels, teachers often give learners a pre-set list of questions and have learners to interview one or more classmates using those questions.

At more advanced levels, learners can create and ask their own questions; you could simply provide a handout that indicates the type of questions or number of questions a student should ask, or write that information on the board.

When students create their own questions, surveys become an opportunity for more open discussion, which helps learners discover a variety of opinions about the reading themes, characters, or events.

To have students begin creating a survey, let them come up with a few survey questions and write those questions on the board. For example, if you were reading a story about a young woman forced to choose between telling the truth or betraying a friend's trust, you might ask students to think of personal questions related to that theme (*Is it better to tell the truth or better to be quiet?*).

31

SKITS ON READING

Dramatization can be an excellent way to increase student motivation, not to mention that it can help students to read, listen, speak, and write!

However, this can be a rather advanced way to teach a reading and requires careful preparation. Consider the following tips/ideas to structure the event:

1. After reading an article or story, have students write a short skit based on that story or a part of the story.
2. Have students to form groups and decide which skit should be dramatized.
3. Students choose the actors and/or narrator for the sketch.
4. Students should work together to produce costumes, props, or other visual items that will make the skit clear and fun.

As a teacher, you might want to provide some simple costume items or props (a hat, a necktie, a phone, a book, etc.)

PICTURE THE STORY

Encourage students to focus on the location of a story by having them draw from their imagination the neighborhood (or other setting) in which the story takes place. It is helpful to tell students to think of this story as a movie: how would a scene get filmed? What would it look like? This is a particularly good activity for visual learners and those with creative talents.

While you can always have students draw or color on a regular-sized piece of paper, you might get creative and invite students to use the entire whiteboard, paint a mural on a blank wall, or create poster-sized visuals of different scenes.

Although this activity naturally allows students to demonstrate their reading comprehension, you can further their English skills by having students describe their own drawings either in writing or as a presentation.

MIX AND MATCH
(CONCENTRATION)

Write 15-20 of words (such as target vocabulary from a reading the class has done, or one you're preparing them for) on cards, and for each one, create a matching card with picture or definition. Create one complete set of cards for every group of 4-6 students.

For example, if the word on one card is *skyscraper*, the matching card will have a picture or definition of the word *skyscraper*.

Place the word cards and picture cards face down on a table, in two groups. Students take turns selecting one card from each group and turning them over. If they match, the student keeps the cards. If they don't match, the cards are placed back face down.

Continue taking turns until all pairs have been matched. The student with the most matching pairs wins the game.

❧ 34 ❧

FLYSWATTER

Place a number of vocabulary words on cards on a large table (you can use either images or written words). Divide students into two teams. Have each team line up single file at a table. The first student in each line is given a flyswatter. Read a definition of one of the words; the first student to hit the word with the flyswatter takes that card for his/her team as a 'point.'

The winner hands the flyswatter to the next person in line. The student who misses gets two more chances, and then also passes the flyswatter to the next person in line. Continue until all cards are gone.

Variation: Write the words on the board, and have students swat them there.

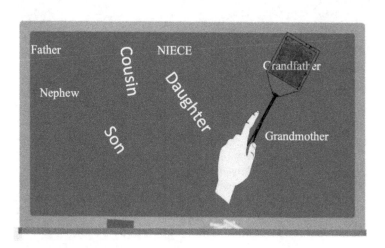

THE TRAIN

This activity allows students to work together to communicate a single message. It is often done in two or more teams.

Divide students into even-numbered groups. Each group forms a line, often a row of chairs or desks, leading from the back of the class to the front. The front of the class should have a whiteboard or other place to write an answer.

Each "train" consists of an engine (one student at the front of the class), a group of cars (any number of students in the middle), and a caboose (a student at the back of the class).

Tell students that you will talk only to the caboose of each team, and that each member of the team can only speak to the person directly in front of them (they must all whisper into the ear of the next "car").

To begin the game, go to a place where no one can hear and either whisper or show in writing a sentence from the reading that you want each team to write on the board. The "caboose" goes back to the train and whispers to the person directly in front of them.

When each car has communicated the message to the person in front, the engine (the final car) must then write the correct sentence on the board. The "train" that writes the correct word on the board first wins.

❦ IV ❦
INTENSIVE ACTIVITIES

Intensive activities aim to help students dive into the particulars of a reading text. In other words, intensive activities invite students to focus in on particular details or perhaps a particular strategy to comprehend the text, rather than focusing on the general meaning of an entire passage. Intensive activities might concentrate on a particular grammar concept, for example, or perhaps have students focus on a single character, plot point, or location within the text.

Often an intensive activity is chosen only after an objective is considered first. In other words, if you are hoping to help students learn about the city of Gettysburg during the time of the Civil War, then you could have students scan for references to the place itself within a particular passage, lifting only the parts that pertain to the city and ignoring other information that might be pertinent for another search.

You may, however, wish to focus on a group of difficult vocabulary words; then a scavenger hunt or scramble might be more appropriate. In this section I'll present a number of commonly used intensive activities that cover a wide range of purposes.

❧ 36 ❧
SKIMMING

Skimming is a tool that gets students to read in order to capture a general view of a passage or reading. Skimming refers to looking only for the general or main ideas, and works best with non-fiction (or factual) material.

Often students are invited to skim BEFORE they read, making the exercise a prediction activity worthy of a class-room discussion (*Skim for two minutes and then discuss what you learned so far with a partner*).

With skimming, your overall understanding is reduced, which may cause anxiety for some students. However, having a purpose for a skimming activity reduces that anxiety quite a bit. For example, you might ask them to answer some simple questions about the reading that they could skim for:

- How many pages long is the article?
- Are there any graphs, charts, or illustrations?
- Is the tone humorous or serious?

- Are there any quotes from experts?

Skimming also teaches learners to pay particular attention to major organizational markers, so you could have them look specifically for topic sentences, introductions and conclusions, and key ideas such as those indicated by bolded text.

SCANNING

Scanning is often confused with the previous activity (Skimming; tip #36), but is actually quite different.

While both skimming and scanning can be useful tools for speeding up reading, with skimming you generally look for main ideas and overall meaning.

When scanning, however, learners look for a specific piece of information, just as one might look for a specific flight at an airport terminal, or a favorite team's scores in the newspaper.

The most common iteration of this activity invites students to scan by simply writing up a few specific questions on the board (dates, names, and numbers work particularly well).

Another way to elicit scanning is by asking learners to find a key word or idea that appears somewhere in the passage, telling them that they have permission to not read everything.

To increase speed and engage in a bit of student movement, one variation on scanning is to have students stand up as they read, and sit down once they have found the answers—however, don't leave just one or two students standing, which could embarrass them; when most of the class has finished, let everyone sit down.

PREFIX/SUFFIX SCAVENGER HUNT

]Intensive activities are often used to teach a particular set of vocabulary words that are deemed the "important" words for a text. Important words are often chosen because they are

1. words that must be understood for the text to be understood
2. words that must be learned for students to become more proficient in their English level in general
3. words that will appear elsewhere in other readings or material.

One way to target the learning of key words in a reading is to prepare a list of vocabulary words directly from the reading but by providing these words in unique ways: for example, with different suffixes or prefixes. In other words, the words given may share the same root but may be transformed in some way that is relevant and worthy of discussion.

Students can then identify the word in the text and match it to the word in the vocabulary word bank. A teacher could explain any change in meaning due to the transformation of the word, and help students practice recognizing roots, prefixes, and suffixes.

SINGLE WORD SCRAMBLE

]Many teachers want to focus on key vocabulary by providing fill-in-the-blank exercises. This exercise is similar to those but perhaps a little bit more fun.

In this intensive activity, a teacher chooses vocabulary words directly from the reading, just like you would for the more typical exercises. But rather than providing a definition and creating a space for students to choose the correct answer, you might provide the definition and jumble the individual words so that students can guess at and unscramble each word ('scramble' becomes *scmblra*).

For variety, you might consider a scrambling competition by inviting two students to the board, writing a scrambled version of the word, and letting the students compete to solve the scrambled word most quickly. If students get stuck on a difficult word, give hints about its meaning.

SENTENCE SCRAMBLE

When certain sentences are particularly relevant to a reading—often because they highlight key concepts or vocabulary—consider using a sentence scramble. This activity focuses attention on those key concepts and/or vocabulary words, and also reinforces students' awareness and understanding of syntax.

First, choose one or more of these important sentences; take them directly from the reading.

Necessity is the mother of invention.

Second, put the words in a jumbled order. Create a work-sheet with all of the jumbled sentences, or write them on the board. You can decide if you want to leave in clues like capital letters to signal the first word in the sentence or not.

Necessity is the mother of invention becomes *invention the of Necessity mother is*

Third, have students unscramble the words and check their answers with a partner. As a follow-up, see if they can remember where in the reading they encountered the sentences, and check that they understand both the meaning and the importance of the sentences.

PARAGRAPH SCRAMBLE

A paragraph scramble is just like the word or sentence scramble, but in paragraphs rather than smaller units. Doing a paragraph scramble, however, can have the distinct purpose of inviting students to look at the organization or time sequence of a particular passage.

In order to conduct a paragraph scramble, take several sentences from the reading—for example, 5-6 for beginners, and as many as 10 sentences for advanced learners.

Cut the sentences into equal-sized strips of paper. On the back of these sentence strips, write numbers or letters in a random order. Students are required to put them in correct order. For convenience, the numbers on the back of each sentence can help when discussing the correct order.

For example, one paragraph might have the order 1, 3, 5, 2, 4. Students can compare their answers to the correct order and then move on to the next paragraph scramble. Having 2 or 3 paragraph scrambles per activity is common.

SEPARATION STATION

This activity invites students to pay attention to word form and get a sense of meaning through careful attention to letters and words.

This activity is done by taking sentences from a reading and removing all the spaces. Students then look at the words and separate them out. After they separate them out, you can have them write the sentences on the board.

Alternatively, you could have students share their sentences aloud with a partner. In other words, you should think about whether this could be turned into a writing or a speaking activity.

Students who learn to parse sentences in this fashion improve their ability to identify words within sentences. As a follow-on activity, you could have students identify all the nouns, verbs, etc. found within the sentence.

EXAMPLE

IthinkthatIwouldreallyenjoyvisitingParisespeciallytheEiffel-Tower

Answer: *I think that I would really enjoy visiting Paris, especially the Eiffel Tower.*

43

PUNCTUATION STATION

This activity looks quite similar to the previous activity (#42, Separation Station), however it is distinct in that it focuses on punctuation and capitalization.

Again, take a few sentences from a reading and remove all spaces, but this time, also remove punctuation and capital letters. Tell students to add all necessary punctuation and capitalization. Then, once again, invite students to share sentences on the board or turn it into a speaking activity.

As a variation, you might want to invite two or more students to share their sentences on the board, and compare any differences that they might have.

For added complexity, you could create an entire paragraph's worth of sentences and then have students parse out all of the sentences that they find.

EXAMPLE

ithinkthatiwouldreallyenjoyvisitingpariswhatcitydoy-
ouwanttovisit

Answer: *I think that I would really enjoy visiting Paris. What city do you want to visit?*

❧ 44 ❧

SYNONYM MATCH

Synonym matching is yet another intensive activity that involves a word bank. As in our previous activities, take a group of key words from key sentences. If you are doing a worksheet, you might create a word bank in the upper left hand corner.

Now create an alternate word bank in the upper right hand corner with synonyms. Have learners connect the key word with the appropriate synonym in a simple matching exercise.

A variation on this particular activity is to provide only the synonyms (that is, only the left-hand word bank) and pull entire sentences from the passage with the key words. Key words are bolded within each sentence. Students then exchange the bolded word with the synonym match.

❧ 45 ❧

SPACED REPETITION

A lot of research in vocabulary and language learning has demonstrated that learners often forget what they have studied, and that learners fail to acquire vocabulary with repeated practice over time. Spaced repetition is one strategy that addresses that concern.

Have learners make flashcards and place them in 5 boxes. Invite them to review these flashcards at intervals. Tell students that all the cards begin in box 3, but if they answer a card correctly, it goes "one box up" (meaning from 3 to 4, or 4 to 5), and if it is answered incorrectly, it goes "one box down" (meaning from 3 to 2 or 2 to 1).

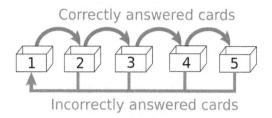

Have students review the cards

- in box 5 every day
- in box 4, every two days
- in box 3 every 4 days
- box 2 every 5 days,
- in box 1 every week.

Thus, incorrectly answered cards are practiced more often, and correctly answered cards are practiced less.

❦ 46 ❧
REBUS

A rebus strip replaces words with clip art or images, giving students a chance to practice vocabulary by reading aloud the word every time they see the image.

For example, instead of the word *chicken*, replace the word with a small image of a chicken (like an emoji) and ask students to say aloud the word, just as they do the regular words, when they encounter the image.

Example:

My uncle has two s.

(My uncle has two chickens.)

A rebus strip can be read in pairs or as a group with the teacher. Students can also form their own rebus and read it aloud in class.

A variation on the rebus strip can be done by having students replace words within a story with their own actions or ideas. A teacher, reading a story aloud, could ask students to replace key words (especially verbs like *jump/laugh*, nouns like *mouse* or adjectives like *cold* or *hilarious*) with a pantomimed action. Students enjoy anticipating a teacher's prompt and predicting the correct answer.

❧ V ❧

EXTENSIVE ACTIVITIES

Have you ever met a teacher that loved handing out books? Favorite, worn-out books that students from years past have checked out and read? You can often spot an extensive reading teacher by the vast library he or she has collected over the years. An extensive reading teacher asks questions about what students like, and matches different readers with different texts.

But what is extensive reading?

Extensive reading refers to a series of aims and techniques that allow readers to be exposed to large quantities of text. While intensive techniques are used to have students focus in on a small portion of a text (a word, a group of words, a sentence, a paragraph), extensive techniques are used to encourage students to read large amount of text—for example, entire novels—and, eventually, enjoy reading more.

In other words, the goal of extensive reading is principally enjoyment and meaning. Extensive reading promotes vocabulary acquisition, reading speed, and reading fluency. Those who read a lot, get lost in reading, and love reading, are often bound for reading success. Confidence, success, and motivation are at the core of the extensive reading program.

47

READING LOGS

One of the most common motivational techniques is a reading log, often placed proudly somewhere within the room. A reading log allows students to show each other what they are reading outside class (or inside, if you have private reading time).

There should be a set time each week when students share with each other what they read. They can write down answers to questions, discuss what they liked about what they read, ask questions to others who have read the same book, or whatever you would like to have them do in the reading log.

A reading log simply means that you invite students to engage in what they are reading. One reading teacher I know uses a reading log to help students use the vocabulary they learned in the reading. This teacher asks students to write sentences using the words they did not know before reading. Another reading teacher invites students to write a story based on a minor character, or write as if they were one of the characters.

48

READING ZONES

Setting up a reading zone is a way of creating a comfortable space for learners. A reading zone might be an entirely separate room at some schools, where reading in English is encouraged. There might also be movies and games to encourage language learning; but the concept of a reading zone is that it serves primarily as a comfortable place where students can read.

This is different from a library, although having a healthy library can help students select a wide variety of books that encourage them to read.

The zone should feel like a space in which students can "let their hair down" and relax. Beanbag chairs, comfortable couches, shelves filled with books, colorful posters, and even competition charts (where students log the number of books or number of pages read in a certain time frame) to encourage students to outperform each other can be elements of a reading zone.

Variation: Encourage students to set up a reading zone in their own homes or another place they know. A reading zone can be as small as a favorite comfortable chair by a window. Have students bring in photos of their reading zones to share with a group or the class.

❦ 49 ❦

PICTURE BOOKS

Most people are familiar with picture books—illustrated books created by an author, generally for younger readers.

However, this activity involves having students create their own picture books. After students listen to a story, or when they choose a favorite story they have heard, letting students be in charge of the creation of their own picture book can be quite motivational.

One way to do this activity is to assign a book or short story to read. Another way is to have students choose from a list of famous fables or stories, or even choose a favorite story on their own.

After the selection of a story, have each student create series of pictures (perhaps no more than 10) about the story. Students must summarize their story so that it fits the correct number of pictures, and storyboard the ideas and illustrate them in a way that makes the story take shape and come to life.

After students finish, have them summarize their story to a partner or to the class.

BOOK REPORTS

A book report allows students to express their opinions and feelings about a reading, and is often done in conjunction with extensive reading. In other words, students are invited to choose their own book—something that interests them—read it, and then respond to it.

A book report generally consists of a summary of the main ideas of the reading and a reflection on what was learned/enjoyed. Often a teacher creates a form, and there are hundreds of templates available online.

However, a book report can also be much more. It can be an exploration of a favorite character or a description of the setting, the historical background, or other details from the reading. It could also include a short discussion of a favorite scene and any number of questions you wish to ask in the book report. You might ask students to discuss how easy or challenging the reading was, how they handled new vocabulary they encountered, and whether they would recommend it to other students in the class.

Sometimes book reports are given orally, with students are given the opportunity to share stories that they particularly loved. Remember, the idea of extensive reading is to encourage others to read, so giving students the opportunity to share their favorite books can be contagious.

BONUS TIP!

51. TEA LEAF READING

If you are ever feeling a bit more adventurous or daring, this activity can go really well, especially if you commit to the silliness of it. It involves a certain amount of acting, so for some of you, this may be easier than for others.

Tea leaf reading goes like this: After reading the first chapter of a story or article, tell students that they will follow the ancient practice of "tea leaf reading," by first drinking some "tea" (it can be water or any drink) and then compete to see who is the better predictor of the future events in the reading.

Have students take cups in some sort of solemn ceremony, perhaps even with a shared chant or closed eyes. Then have students open their eyes and begin to predict.

To help students predict, a teacher might have a number of sentence starters: For example, *Even though John is nervous about joining the basketball team...*

ABOUT THE AUTHOR

Dr. Shane Dixon, Senior International Educator, Arizona State University, has 20 years of TESOL experience, and has taught in Venezuela, Mexico, Iraq, and the US. He has helped designed teacher training programs for groups from China, Korea, Japan, Iraq, Peru, and Mexico, and has created language programs for companies such as General Electric (Brazil), LG (Korea), and Toyota (Japan).

He is also the creator of the popular series *Teach English Now!* from Arizona State University, the largest TESOL Certificate program in world (available on www.coursera.org).

He holds a doctorate in educational technology from Arizona State University and a master's degree in English (with an emphasis in language planning and policy) from Brigham Young University.

Dr. Dixon is the author of *100 TESOL Activities: Practical ESL/EFL Activities for the Communicative Classroom*, and *The Language Learner Guidebook: Powerful Tools to Conquer Any Language*.

~

ABOUT THE SERIES

Teaching English as a second or foreign language is full of challenges: How do you hold students' interest? How do you ensure that they get enough practice to really learn?

The *Fifty Ways to Teach* series gives you a variety of drills, games, techniques, methods, and ideas to help your students master English. Most of the ideas can be used for both beginning and advanced classes. Many require little to no preparation or special materials.

The ideas can be used with any textbook, or without a textbook at all. These short, practical guides aim to make your teaching life easier, and your students' lives more rewarding and successful.

Note: We have priced these *50 Ways to Teach* books very cheaply, because we want education and learning to be available to as many people as possible, and have made them available in both print and ebook form.

However, our authors are highly qualified professionals who

work hard to create these books. If these books are useful to you, please recommend them to your friends—but please do not share them freely. Our authors will continue to write excellent and cheap books for you if they make a little money. That way, we all win. Thank you for your support!

If you have comments or suggestions (such as ideas for future books that you would find useful), feel free to contact the publisher at editor@wayzgoosepress.com, check out the offerings on our publishing website at http://wayzgoosepress.com.